Table of Contents

What Are Reindeer?

Reindeer are large mammals.
They are members of the deer
family. In some places,
reindeer are called caribou.

Reindeer are different from
other kinds of deer. Both males
and females have antlers.

Reindeer can range in color from dark brown to almost completely white.

Size

Adult reindeer are usually between four and five feet tall at the shoulder. They can weigh up to 700 pounds.

Reindeer that live in the wild are taller than reindeer that are **domesticated**. They often have longer legs.

Male reindeer are usually

larger and heavier than

female reindeer.

Physical Characteristics

Reindeer have two layers of fur. The bottom layer is thick and helps to keep them warm. The top layer is thinner and allows reindeer to float in the water.

Their nostrils also help to keep them warm. Their shape allows them to warm the air that reindeer breathe.

Their hooves are large and have two toes. This helps them to walk through the snow, wetlands, and swim.

Antlers

Reindeer have large antlers. They use them to fight with other reindeer and to dig through snow.

Their antlers grow from two points on their head. When they first grow in, they are covered in a soft velvet. The velvet dries up and reindeer rub their antlers on trees to remove it.

Reindeer shed their antlers each year. They will grow back again later. When they grow back, they are bigger than before.

Habitat

Reindeer are found in woodlands, mountains, and the **tundra**.

Their habitats are much farther north than other kinds of deer. Their **adaptations** allow them to live in areas where it is very cold.

Range

Reindeer are found in North America, Europe, and Asia.

Most reindeer are found in

Norway, Alaska, Siberia, and

Greenland.

Diet

Reindeer are **herbivores**. This means that they eat only plants.

Their diet is made up of moss, lichen, herbs, grass, and leaves. It often depends on the season.

Reindeer have a great sense of

smell. They can smell food

through the snow.

In the winter, less food is available. Reindeer eat a lot of lichen and moss. They have also be known to eat small animals such as lemmings if food is **scarce**.

Reindeer are thought to enjoy eating mushrooms.

Reindeer can eat up to eighteen pounds of food each day. They have to spend a lot of time **grazing** to get enough food.

Communication

Reindeer use sound, scent, and movement to communicate with each other.

They are known to use sound more than other members of the deer family. They may grunt, snort, and roar.

Reindeer may stomp their hooves or **thrust** their antlers at another reindeer. This is a sign of **aggression**.

Movement

Reindeer have been known to run up to fifty miles per hour. They need to be fast to escape **predators** such as wolves.

Reindeer are good swimmers. They often swim to cross rivers. The shape of their hooves helps them to swim.

Reindeer have been known to **migrate** over 3,000 miles in a year.

Reindeer Calves

Reindeer usually have one baby but can sometimes have twins. Baby reindeer are called calves.

Reindeer calves are different from other kinds of deer. They do not have spotted fur when they are born.

When they are first born, calves do not have antlers. They will start to grow points after about two years.

Herd Life

Reindeer are social animals. They live in groups that are called herds. A herd can have between ten and one hundred reindeer.

Herds travel south in the winter, protect calves, and look for food together.

Sometimes, several herds come together and form a super herd.

Super herds can be made up of over 10,000 reindeer.

Helping People

In some areas of the Arctic, people have reindeer has **livestock**. They can provide people with milk, meat, and fur.

Reindeer are also kept to help people. They are strong and can pull heavy loads.

Reindeer are often used to pull sleds. They help people to get around in areas where there is a lot of snow.

Population

Reindeer are listed as **vulnerable**.

Their populations are **declining**

all over the world. If this

continues, they could become

endangered.

Warmer temperatures, disease,

and habitat loss are the main

threats that reindeer are facing.

Reindeer can live up to fifteen

years in the wild.

Helping Reindeer

People are trying to help reindeer populations by preserving their habitats. They want to make sure reindeer have a safe habitat to live in.

Reindeer are often hunted for their meat. There are hunting laws that help to protect reindeer populations.

Warmer temperatures and **tourism** are affecting reindeer habitats. Their habitats are getting smaller.

Many people want to try to stop the change in temperature so that reindeer habitats are not destroyed. They also want to limit tourism to preserve habitats.

Glossary

Adaptation: a feature that helps animals to survive

Aggression: the use of force or violence

Declining: getting smaller

Domesticated: tame

Endangered: at risk of becoming extinct

Grazing: to feed on growing grass

Herbivore: an animal that eats only plants

Livestock: animals raised by people and kept on a farm or ranch

Migrate: when animals move from one place to another

Predator: an animal that hunts other animals for food

Scarce: when there is little available

Thrust: to push

Tourism: when people travel to an area for entertainment

Tundra: the plains areas of the Arctic

Vulnerable: an animal that may become endangered

About the Author

Victoria Blakemore is a first grade

teacher in Southwest Florida with a

passion for reading.

You can visit her at

www.enchantedinelementary.com

Copyright info/picture credits

Cover, Andreas Gradin/AdobeStock; Page 3, Mariamichelle/Pixabay; Page 5, Natalia_Kollegova/Pixabay; Page 7, MAKY_OREL/Pixabay; Page 9, Natalia_Kollegova/Pixabay; Page 11, skeeze/Pixabay; Pages 12-13, LTapsaH/Pixabay; Page 15, Natalia_Kollegova/Pixabay; Page 17, Natalia_Kollegova/Pixabay; Page 19, Aliba59/Pixabay; Page 21, skeeze/Pixabay; Page 23; belov3097/AdobeStock; Page 25, broesis/Pixabay; Page 27, ennymore/Pixabay; Page 29, Natalia_Kollegova/Pixabay; Page 31, L0nd0ner/Pixabay; Page 33, Andreas Gradin/AdobeStock

Also in This Series

CPSIA information can be obtained
at www.ICGtesting.com
Printed in the USA
LVOW06*1547241117
557328LV00023B/358/P

9 781947 439450